Where Is
Washington?

W0114223

Where Is Washington?

by Tracy Vonder Brink

illustrated by Ted Hammond

Penguin Workshop

For all the kids in Washington—TVB

PENGUIN WORKSHOP
An imprint of Penguin Random House LLC
1745 Broadway, New York, NY 10019
penguinrandomhouse.com

Copyright © 2026 by Penguin Random House LLC

Penguin Random House values and supports copyright. Copyright fuels creativity,
encourages diverse voices, promotes free speech, and creates a vibrant culture. Thank you
for buying an authorized edition of this book and for complying with copyright laws by not
reproducing, scanning, or distributing any part of it in any form without permission. You
are supporting writers and allowing Penguin Random House to continue to publish books
for every reader. Please note that no part of this book may be used or reproduced in any
manner for the purpose of training artificial intelligence technologies or systems.

PENGUIN is a registered trademark and PENGUIN WORKSHOP is a trademark
of Penguin Books Ltd. WHO HQ & Design is a registered trademark of
Penguin Random House LLC.

Designed and Produced by Dinardo Design, LLC.

Library of Congress Cataloging-in-Publication Data is available.

First published in the United States of America by Penguin Workshop, 2026

Manufactured in the United States of America
CJKW

ISBN 9798217053377 (paperback)
10 9 8 7 6 5 4 3 2 1

ISBN 9798217053384 (library binding)
10 9 8 7 6 5 4 3 2 1

The authorized representative in the EU for product safety and compliance is
Penguin Random House Ireland, Morrison Chambers, 32 Nassau Street,
Dublin D02 YH68, Ireland, https://eu-contact.penguin.ie.

Contents

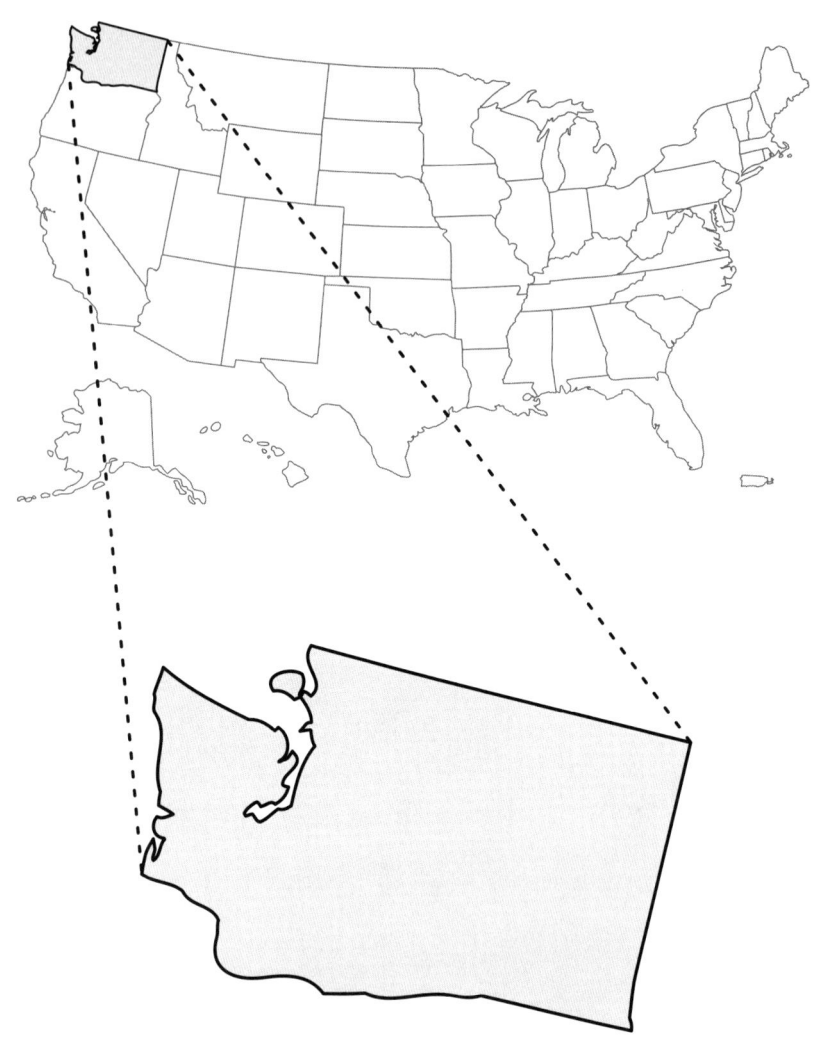

Where Is Washington?

The Puyallup (say: pew-AL-up) Nation calls one of Washington's most famous mountains "Loowitlatkla" (say: LOO-wit-LAT-kla)—"Lady of Fire"—for good reason. It's no ordinary mountain. It's also a volcano. (A British explorer named it Mount St. Helens in 1792.) In 1980, it had been mostly quiet for more than one hundred years. That spring, Mount St. Helens rumbled with small earthquakes for weeks. The Lady of Fire was about to wake up.

On May 18, 1980, a 5.1-magnitude quake shook Mount St. Helens. Its northern side collapsed and caused the largest landslide ever recorded. As the side of the mountain fell away, it released gases that had built up inside. It was like opening a shaken-up can of soda. The blast flattened 230 miles of forest and shot out hot rocks, ash, and steam. The tower of ash rose 18 miles in the air. Mount St. Helens spewed 540 million tons of ash over 22,000 square miles.

The air temperature reached 660 degrees Fahrenheit. The heat melted snow and ice. Water mixed with the ash and created huge mudflows, called lahars. The lahars destroyed more than 185 miles of roads and over 200 homes.

The eruption lasted more than nine hours. By the time it was over, fifty-seven people had died. Most were campers and hikers who thought they were far enough away from the mountain to be safe. Mount St. Helens had been 9,677 feet high. After the eruption, it was down to 8,365 feet. More than 1,300 feet of Mount St. Helens had blown off. Mount St. Helens is the most active volcano in Washington, but it's not the only one. Volcanoes have been erupting there for the past thirty-six million years!

CHAPTER 1
Welcome to Washington

Washington is full of natural wonders. It has tall mountains, green forests, and rainy shores. Sitting in the northwestern corner of the United States, its total area is 71,300 square miles, making it the eighteenth-largest US state. The state is 240 miles long and 360 miles wide. British Columbia, a part of Canada, lies to its north. Idaho borders the state to the east and Oregon to the south. The Pacific Ocean meets Washington's western coast.

Washington has more than three thousand named mountains, making it one of the most mountainous states. Ice and snow are found on almost all of its tallest mountains. Some receive between four hundred and seven hundred inches of snow every year. It's one of the snowiest places on earth! Washington also has more than three hundred glaciers (large areas of ice that last all year). It has more glaciers than any state but Alaska.

The Cascade Range is Washington's largest. The Cascades are also one of North America's major mountain ranges. Mount Rainier (say: ray-NEAR) is the highest mountain in the Cascades and in Washington. It's 14,410 feet tall! It's also an active volcano. Four other active volcanoes—

Mount St. Helens, Glacier Peak, Mount Baker, and Mount Adams—are also in the Cascades.

The Cascades separate the state into Western and Eastern Washington. More than half of the state's residents make their homes on its western side, between the Cascades and the coast. This fifty-mile-wide region, called the Western Lowlands, is the most densely populated part of the state. The cities of Seattle, Tacoma, and Everett are in this area. They sit along the shores

of the Puget (say: PEW-jit) Sound, a ninety-five-mile-long estuary (an area where a freshwater river meets the sea) that connects to the Pacific Ocean.

The waters of Puget Sound are home to humpback whales, sea lions, and sea otters, plus hundreds of kinds of seabirds. Southern Resident killer whales spend summer and fall months there every year. This population of orcas are made up of three family groups, called pods, and are only found in the Pacific Northwest.

The Olympic Peninsula lies across from Puget Sound. This peninsula (a piece of land almost surrounded by water) covers 3,600 miles and includes the Olympic Mountains. The Olympic Peninsula has four temperate rain forests. Temperate rainforests have much cooler temperatures than tropical rainforests, but they're just as wet. Washington's Hoh (say: HOE) Rainforest receives almost twelve feet of rain per year. That's more than the Amazon jungle!

The state's western side is rainy, but its eastern side is said to enjoy up to three hundred days of sunshine every year. Eastern Washington has many different types of landscapes, including foothills (low hills at the base of a mountain), lakes, and sand dunes. The Columbia Plateau was formed by lava ten to fifteen million years ago. It's the world's second-largest lava plateau. Today, more than three hundred crops are grown in its rich soil. Spokane (say: spo-CAN), Washington's second-largest city, is in Eastern Washington.

Some of North America's oldest human remains have been found in the southeastern part of the state. The bones are about ten thousand years old! The cave where they were found was named the Marmes Rockshelter after the farmer who owned the land. Archaeologists think ancient people used the cave as a sort of home base. They also buried some of their dead there. We don't know who these people were or what they called themselves, but they left behind thousands of artifacts (objects made by ancient people), including tools made from animal bones.

The relatives of those ancient people spread throughout what later became Washington. Tens of thousands of Indigenous people had been living in the Puget Sound area for thousands of years by the time European and American settlers arrived. They belonged to many nations, including the Suquamish (say: soo-QUA-mish), Duwamish (say: doo-WAH-mish), Nisqually (say: nis-QUA-lee), Snoqualmie (say: SNOW-kwal-mee), Chinook, Muckleshoot, and Puyallup Nations.

These nations spoke different dialects (ways of speaking) of a language family called Salish (say: SAY-lish). They built villages of large wooden houses along rivers and coasts. From spring to fall every year, millions of salmon swam to these waters to lay eggs. The fish were a food source and something they could trade, but ceremonies such as the First Salmon Feast were also part of the nations' religion. The fish were so important to the nations that they called themselves The Salmon People. They still do!

In 1803, the United States bought the land between the Mississippi River and the Rocky Mountains from France in a deal called the Louisiana Purchase, even though Indigenous nations were already living there. A year later, the US government sent Meriwether Lewis and William Clark to explore the territory and look for a route to the Pacific Ocean. Lewis and Clark led an expedition (a trip made by a group for a specific purpose) of thirty to forty people, including York, an enslaved Black man. York hunted to feed everyone on the expedition. Sacagawea (say: sah-KAH-gah-WEE-ah) was a member of the Shoshone (say: show-SHOW-nee) Nation. She may have been born in Idaho, but historians aren't sure. She and her husband, a French Canadian fur trapper, joined the expedition. Sacagawea helped Lewis and Clark communicate with the Indigenous people they met.

The Lewis and Clark Expedition traveled through what is now Washington from October 1805 to May 1806. They paddled their canoes down the Snake River and into the Columbia River. Along the way, they met many Indigenous nations, including the Chinook, who were already trading with European ships that landed on the coast. Lewis and Clark took notes about the peoples they met. They wrote down the names of the nations and where they lived. Clark made maps of everywhere they went.

In 1818, Great Britain and the United States shared the Oregon Country, an area that stretched between the Rocky Mountains and the Pacific Ocean. Starting in the 1840s, American settlers moved west in search of jobs and land. They traveled by wagon over a route called the Oregon Trail to reach what are now Oregon, Washington, Utah, and California. The two-thousand-mile trip took between four and six months.

Puget Sound's First American Settlers

In the mid-1800s, the Oregon Trail was more than a path: It was a rugged journey across the Rocky Mountains to the West. Although it was dangerous, many Americans set out in covered wagons in search of a different future. In 1844, the first group of Americans to settle what is today Puget Sound did just that.

George Bush was a Black man who brought his family and four others to what is now Oregon in hopes of finding a new home. But a law said Black people could not settle in the area. The other families didn't want to stay where Bush and his family couldn't, so the group moved near Puget Sound.

George Bush

Bush and the others founded Tumwater, the first American settlement in Puget Sound. Bush also built a successful farm near what is now Olympia. (Today, some of that land is still called Bush Prairie.) He and his family were friends with members of the Nisqually Nation who lived nearby and learned their language. Bush also helped new settlers by giving them food until they could grow their own.

William, his oldest son, later became the first Black person to serve in the Washington legislature. William Bush introduced the bill that founded Washington State University. The Bush family was a groundbreaking part of Washington history.

In 1846, the United States and Great Britain signed the Oregon Treaty (an agreement between countries). It gave the United States the area that would one day become Oregon, Washington, Idaho, and parts of Montana and Wyoming. They believed they had a right to take the land from Indigenous peoples by force, even though the Indigenous peoples had lived there for thousands of years. The treaty also established the border between the United States and Canada.

The Oregon Treaty had given one strait (a narrow passage of water) to the United States and one to Great Britain. The San Juan Islands lay between the two straits. Both countries claimed the islands, and settlers from both countries lived there. Three years after the treaty was signed, a pig belonging to a British company tore up an American farmer's garden. The farmer killed the pig, and the British threatened to kick all the American settlers off the islands. An American commander sent soldiers to protect the settlers. A British commander sent warships. It looked like the countries might go to war over a pig!

US president James Buchanan (say: bu-CAN-non) didn't want war. He sent General Winfield Scott to talk to the British commanders. They agreed to keep the peace. Twelve years later, the United States and Great Britain finally signed a treaty that gave the San Juan Islands to the Americans.

CHAPTER 2
Becoming a State

Members of the Suquamish and Duwamish Nations had been living in the area around Puget Sound for thousands of years. Around 1810, Chief Si'ahl (say: SEE-ah-lsch) became the leader of both nations. He was respected as a peacemaker. When the first American settlers reached Puget Sound around 1852, Si'ahl welcomed them. He became friends with David Maynard, who opened a store in the new town of Duwumps. Maynard named his store the "Seattle Exchange" in honor of his friend. (Seattle is an Americanized version of Si'ahl.)

The land around Puget Sound was different from what settlers were used to. Thick forests had to be cleared to make farms. Crops they'd planted back east didn't do well in the area's heavy rain. Chief Si'ahl and his people helped the newcomers and showed them how to farm and build homes. In 1853, David Maynard convinced Duwumps' settlers to rename their town Seattle.

That same year, Congress made Washington into a territory. Territorial Governor Isaac I. Stevens visited Seattle in 1854. One settler wrote that Si'ahl gave a speech during Stevens's visit and said, "Let him [the white man] be just and kindly with my people." His words were ignored. The US government wanted the land where the Nisqually, Duwamish, Suquamish, and many more nations had lived for generations.

Territorial Governor Stevens was given the job of forcing the nations to sign treaties that granted their land to the United States. Stevens told the leaders that if they didn't agree, the US government would declare war. The leaders of many nations—including Chief Si'ahl —felt they had no choice. They said they would give up their land and move to reservations (land set aside by the government) if they could keep the right to hunt and fish throughout Washington. Stevens agreed. The treaties gave the United States more than sixty-four million acres of land. The nations were left with less than six million acres broken up into reservations.

The United States wanted Indigenous land not only for settlers but also for railroads. In the 1860s, Congress passed acts that gave land to railroad companies across the country. The Northern Pacific Railway Company received about forty-four million acres to build a railroad from Minnesota to Puget Sound. The company decided to put its Puget Sound station in Tacoma.

Thousands of workers moved dirt, dug tunnels, and laid track. About two-thirds of them were Chinese immigrants. They worked longer hours and were paid less than white workers.

They also had to live in separate camps. After the railroad was finished, some Chinese workers stayed in Washington and made it their home.

Many Chinese immigrants found jobs in fish canneries (factories where food is canned) along the Columbia River. Nearly three thousand people worked there by the 1880s. They cleaned

and packed salmon sold in markets around the
world. In just one year, workers in one cannery
packed 272,000 pounds of salmon! Japanese and
Filipino immigrants also moved to Washington
to work in the canneries, on the railroads, and
in logging camps. Although Chinese, Japanese,
and Filipino workers were an important part of

Washington's companies, they were paid less than white workers and faced racism and laws that limited their rights.

The Northern Pacific and other railroads built in Washington changed the territory. The lumber industry boomed as the new railroads carried loads of wood to be sold across the United States. Everett began as a logging camp and grew into a town. Tacoma became one of the world's largest lumber cities of the time.

Cross-country trips that used to take months by wagon could be done in a week or two by train. The Northern Pacific Railway Company ran ads in the United States and in Europe that promoted Washington as a place where workers and farmers could find a better life. Immigrants poured in. Spokane grew faster than any other US city at the time.

Railroads also helped Washington become a state. The lack of roads through the Cascades had made travel between Eastern and Western Washington difficult. The territory's two sides stayed mostly separate until 1887, when a new railroad connected them. Washingtonians soon wanted their territory to become a state. It became the forty-second state in 1889!

Railroads brought new people to Seattle, but the Klondike Gold Rush in 1897 helped the city even more. Gold had been discovered along the Klondike River in what is now Canada's Yukon Territory. Seattle's port was a way for miners in search of gold to reach the Yukon. Newspapers advertised the city as the "Gateway to the Gold Fields." Seattle's stores, restaurants, and hotels made money as seventy thousand hopeful miners passed through on their way to the Yukon.

In the 1890s, irrigation (watering crops by human-made ways) solved a problem for farmers east of the Cascades. The weather and soil in the eastern valleys were perfect for growing apples,

but the mountains blocked rain clouds moving across the state. Digging canals (human-made waterways) to carry river water to fields made it possible for farmers to plant big orchards full of apple trees. The first railroad car of apples was shipped from Yakima Valley in 1894. By the early 1900s, Washington was shipping apples around the United States. Today, the state is still the country's top producer of apples.

CHAPTER 3
One Hundred Years of Innovation

Washingtonians dreamed up big ideas and new inventions over the next century. In 1907, Seattle approved plans for a public market where farmers could sell their goods. The market opened in the newly built Pike Place. Farmers sold out in minutes on its first day. Today, Pike Place Market hosts hundreds of farmers, crafters, and other small businesses and is one of the country's oldest public markets.

The same year Pike Place Market opened, nineteen-year-old Jim Casey and his friend Claude Ryan borrowed one hundred dollars to start the American Messenger Company in Seattle. At first, they delivered packages and messages by bicycle. Casey's company grew to

become the largest delivery service in the city. They wanted the company's vans to stand out and be easy to recognize, so they painted them all the same color—brown. Later, the company name changed to United Parcel Service, or UPS.

In 1915, a businessman named William Boeing (say: BOH-ing) took his first ride in an airplane. He loved it! Even though he owned logging companies, he hired a team and started the Boeing Airplane Co. Soon, the company was making airplanes for the US Navy during World War I. Boeing went on to develop some of the first passenger planes and the jumbo jet.

By 1911, the state government had outgrown its capitol building in Olympia. Construction on the new Washington State Legislative Building, also known as the Capitol Building, began in 1922. It took six years and more than 173 million pounds of stone, brick, concrete, and steel to build. When it was finished, its dome rose 287

feet high. Its dome is the tallest in the United States and one of the tallest in the world.

Washingtonians' new ideas also helped the state's forests. When logging began in the 1800s, companies cut down all the trees in one area and moved on to the next. Starting in the 1930s, the Weyerhaeuser (say: WHERE-houser) Timber Company imagined trees as a crop that could be regrown. In 1941, Weyerhaeuser opened the country's first tree farm. The Clemons Tree Farm launched a movement across the United States to manage forests and grow trees.

Washington also became the home of one of the largest structures ever built by people. Construction on the Grand Coulee Dam on the Columbia River began in 1933. The amount of concrete it took to build the dam would be enough to pave a highway between Seattle and Miami, Florida! When the Grand Coulee Dam opened in 1941, it generated more power than any dam in the United States. It still does!

In 1942, Ruby Inouye Shu (say: in-NO-way shoe) was a student at Washington University. At that time, the United States was fighting Japan in

World War II. The US government forced about 110,000 people of Japanese ancestry to move into internment camps (prison camps during a war). That included Shu, even though she'd been born in Seattle and raised as an American. About thirteen thousand Washingtonians of Japanese ancestry were sent to camps in California, Idaho, and Wyoming. Like Shu, people had to leave schools, jobs, and businesses. Whole families, including children, were given only a week or two to pack their belongings.

Ruby Inouye Shu spent six months in an internment camp in Idaho. Because she'd been a college student, she was allowed to leave and continue her education at the University of Texas. Others weren't so lucky—some were forced to live in the camps until they closed in 1944. Once the government let them leave, some returned to the cities they'd called home. Others moved away. After going to medical school, Shu returned to

Seattle as its first female Japanese American doctor.

In 1948, the US government offered $2,500 to the people who'd been made to live in the camps but did not apologize. Starting in the 1970s, Japanese Americans worked to have the government do more. More than forty years after the war, the US government apologized and gave $20,000 to the people who'd had to live in the camps. Seattle also paid $5,000 to workers who'd been forced to give up their jobs.

Unfair laws also harmed Washington's Indigenous people. Starting in the 1940s, the state said Indigenous people could only fish on their reservations, even though the treaties signed in the 1800s gave them the right to fish anywhere. When Indigenous people tried to fish outside the reservations, they were arrested. Billy Frank Jr., a citizen of the Nisqually Nation, helped organize a protest of two thousand Indigenous people in the state capital. Frank Jr. and members of other nations also held "fish-ins," protests where they fished in areas where they knew they would be arrested. One fish-in held in 1965 lasted six weeks. The arrests were on the news and brought public attention to the loss of Indigenous fishing rights.

The protests and fish-ins continued. In 1970, fourteen of Washington's Indigenous nations sued the state. The judge ruled in favor of the nations and said the 1800s treaties gave them the right to fish where they wanted. The judgment also said Washington had to allow the nations to help manage the state's fisheries (fishing areas controlled by the state). Later, the Supreme Court confirmed the Indigenous nations' fishing rights in Washington. The judgment helped Indigenous nations in other states sue the government for the return of their fishing rights.

As the years passed, Washingtonians continued

to create new products and businesses. Engineers at Boeing's Kent Space Center designed and built lunar rovers, the first vehicles to carry astronauts on the moon. In 1971, the first Starbucks coffee shop opened in Pike Place Market. Bill Gates moved his computer company from New Mexico back to his hometown of Seattle in 1979. By 1990, Microsoft was the first personal computer

software company to reach one billion dollars in sales. Jeff Bezos moved near Seattle in 1994 and started Amazon, the world's first online bookstore, in his garage. Within five years, Amazon had more than $610 million in sales and offered much more than books.

New companies weren't the only thing launched in Washington. In the 1990s, Seattle

bands created a new style of gritty rock music, called grunge. Grunge quickly spread worldwide. Washington bands such as Nirvana, Pearl Jam, and Soundgarden sold millions of records. The kinds of clothes the musical groups wore—such as flannel shirts and ripped jeans bought from thrift stores—became popular. Seattle music and style influenced the whole United States.

CHAPTER 4
The Great State of Washington

Today, nearly eight million people make their homes in Washington. About eight hundred thousand live in Seattle, its largest city. More than two hundred thousand live in both Spokane and Tacoma. Most Washingtonians make their homes in or near its cities. Much of the rest of the state is covered in forests—twenty million acres of trees take up over half the land. These thick evergreen forests are why Washington is known as the Evergreen State.

Washington's population includes more than 140,000 Indigenous people. The US government officially acknowledges twenty-nine Indigenous nations in the state. Seven more nations, including the Duwamish, Wanapum (say: WAH-nuh-pum), and Chinook, have a long history there. Fishing remains important to Indigenous Washingtonians, but they also own businesses. The Yakama Nation is one of the largest employers in the central part of the state.

In addition to its Indigenous peoples, Washington is still home to many descendants of European settlers as well as Black Americans. Immigrants and their descendants from all over the world live in the state. Asian Americans and Pacific Islanders are some of the fastest-growing groups.

Washington has more than thirteen million acres of farmland and over three hundred thousand acres of orchards. It's second in the nation for producing crops! Washington is the number one US producer of blueberries, pears, and sweet cherries. The Walla Walla sweet onion is only grown in the Walla Walla Valley. It became the state vegetable in 2007 after junior high and middle school students and their teachers spent three years writing and emailing the state government.

The state still leads the way in technology. Its companies make more parts for airplanes and spacecraft than any other state. More than half of the satellites flying in low orbit around Earth were built there. Washington is also home to over eighteen thousand information and technology companies. That includes gaming companies— Nintendo of America, Valve, Wizards of the Coast, and Big Fish Games all have their headquarters in the state. The board games Cranium and Pictionary were invented there, too!

Washington's coasts and rivers are still an important part of its economy. The state has nearly seven hundred fishing and seafood companies. It's also the nation's largest producer of farm-raised shellfish. The state of Washington and Indigenous nations co-manage the state's fisheries. They work together to take care of the waters where the fish live, restore fish habitats, and supervise hatcheries where fish and shellfish are raised.

Together, Washingtonians own more than 250,000 watercrafts. That's about one for every five people! They boat, paddle board, windsurf, and much more. The coast has 3,200 miles of

shoreline, some of which is great for scuba diving. Divers may spot the giant Pacific octopus, the world's largest octopus, in the Puget Sound.

Washingtonians enjoy their state's mountains. So do many visitors. More than four million visit its three national parks every year. Some have fun looking for Bigfoot—a tall apelike creature said to

live in the woods. Hikers walk to Colonial Creek Falls in North Cascades National Park. It's the tallest waterfall in the continental United States and the fifteenth tallest in the world! Washington also has more than one hundred state parks with over four hundred miles of trails. In winter, its snowy mountains and trails are perfect for skiing, snowboarding, snowshoeing, and other winter sports.

Other sports are also popular in the state. Seattle is home to the Mariners (Major League Baseball), Seahawks (National Football League), and Kraken (National Hockey League). Every year, Washington University and Washington State's football teams play each other in the Apple Cup. They've been playing against each other since 1900; Washington University leads the series in wins. Gonzaga University's men's basketball team has been in the NCAA tournament every year since 1999. Washingtonians have also brought home thirteen Olympic gold medals. One such Olympian, Megan Rapinoe, played for the Seattle Reign FC (National Women's Soccer League).

Washington brings together natural beauty and innovation. The Evergreen State's forests, mountains, cities, and beaches attract millions of visitors every year. The state has also played an important role in flight, space exploration, and more. Its businesses and music are known around the world. From coffee to computers, Washingtonians have led the way.

Washington at a Glance

Statehood: 1889

Nickname: The Evergreen State

Abbreviation: WA

State Song: "Washington, My Home"

State Tree: Western hemlock

State Animal: Olympic marmot

Capital: Olympia

Size: 71,300 square miles

Population: About 8 million

Famous People from Washington:

Chris Pratt (actor), Brandi Carlile (singer/songwriter), Jimi Hendrix (musician), Ken Jennings (Jeopardy host), Quincy Jones (music producer)

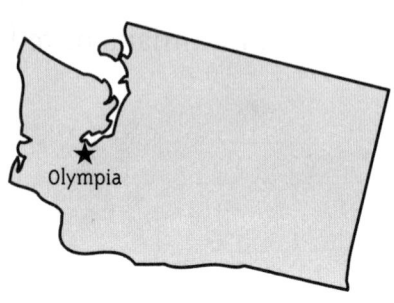

State flag

State bird
Willow goldfinch

State flower
Coast rhododendron

FUN FACT:
Seattle's Space Needle was built for
the 1962 World's Fair. It's 605 feet tall!

Timeline of Washington

10,000–8,000 BCE	Indigenous people bury their dead at Marmes Rockshelter
1805	Lewis and Clark, along with Sacagawea and York, reach the Pacific
1853	Washington becomes a territory
1889	Washington becomes the forty-second US state
1907	Seattle's Pike Place Market opens
1928	Construction of the Washington State Legislative Building is finished
1941	The Grand Coulee Dam opens
1971	A lunar rover built in Kent is used on the moon
1974	Washington's Indigenous nations win a court case and keep their fishing rights
1979	Bill Gates moves Microsoft to Washington
1980	Mount St. Helens erupts
1994	Jeff Bezos launches Amazon near Seattle
2023	More than four million people visit Washington's national parks

Timeline of the World

9,000 BCE	The city of Jericho is built in what is now Palestine
1804	Napoléon Bonaparte becomes emperor of France
1854	Trade opens between Japan and the United States
1887	France begins to build the Eiffel Tower in Paris
1906	Finland is the first European country to give women the right to vote
1928	Penicillin is invented
1945	World War II ends
1972	Richard Nixon is the first US president to visit China
1973	Australia's Sydney Opera House opens
1979	Margaret Thatcher is the first woman to be elected UK prime minister
1980	The *Pac-Man* video game is released in Japan
1994	China begins to build Three Gorges Dam, the world's largest dam
2024	The thirty-third Olympic Games are held in Paris

Bibliography

*Books for young readers

"Animals for Kids." *National Park Service.*
www.nps.gov/mora/learn/kidsyouth/animals-for-kids.htm.

*Barone, Rebecca E.F. *Mountain of Fire: The Eruption and Survivor of Mount St. Helens.* New York: Henry Holt and Company, 2024.

*Fradin, Judith Bloom, and Dennis Brindell Fradin. *Who Was Sacagawea?* New York: Penguin Workshop, 2002.

*Korté, Steve. *What Do We Know About Bigfoot?* New York: Penguin Workshop, 2022.

*Perkins, Hannah. *Washington.* Minneapolis: Abdo Publishing, 2023.

*Sabelko, Rebecca. *Washington.* Minnetonka: Bellwether Media, 2022.

"Washington." *Britannica Kids.*
kids.britannica.com/kids/article/Washington/345535.

"Washington at a Glance." *Britannica Kids.*
kids.britannica.com/kids/article/Washington-at-a-glance/627803.

"Washington Pictures and Facts." *National Geographic Kids.*
kids.nationalgeographic.com/geography/states/article/washington.